Claude gets his claws

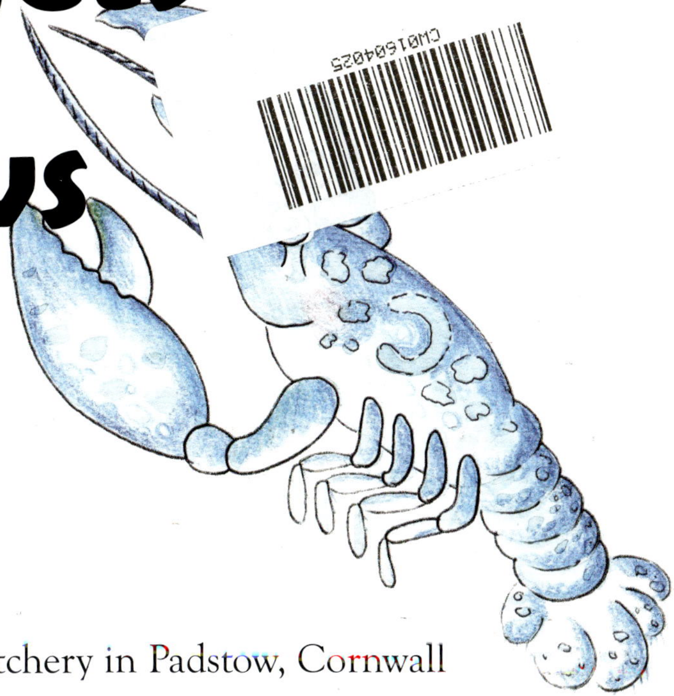

Author: Sarah Boothroyd

Illustrator: Caroline Cleave

Published by the National Lobster Hatchery in Padstow, Cornwall

ISBN: 978-0-9567935-0-8

Max had woken up especially early to set off with Pops – a special day for them both. It was the start of the lobster fishing season and now Max was eight, his mum had agreed he was old enough to go out with Pops to sea; well, just for one day.

It was a cool March morning, the mist rose from Padstow Harbour, drifting through the narrow streets and over the chimney pots. There weren't many people about at five in the morning, just a few local cats prowling the neighbourhood and the seagulls clearing up the scraps left from the previous day.

Max climbed down the ladder and jumped aboard. The engine chugged and spluttered; never a smooth start after a cold winter in the harbour. They were soon off and out into the bay, Max had butterflies in his stomach with excitement.

Can you see the eggs attached to the underside of her belly?

Meanwhile, at the bottom of the sea, in the depths of the ocean, there was a little lobster called Claude, all curled up in his egg, attached to the underside of his mum's tail. He was suddenly aware of being nudged and poked in every direction and there was an increasing amount of noise.

'Budge up Squat.'

'Stop fidgeting Wriggle.'

'Move your legs Titch, I need to stretch out'.

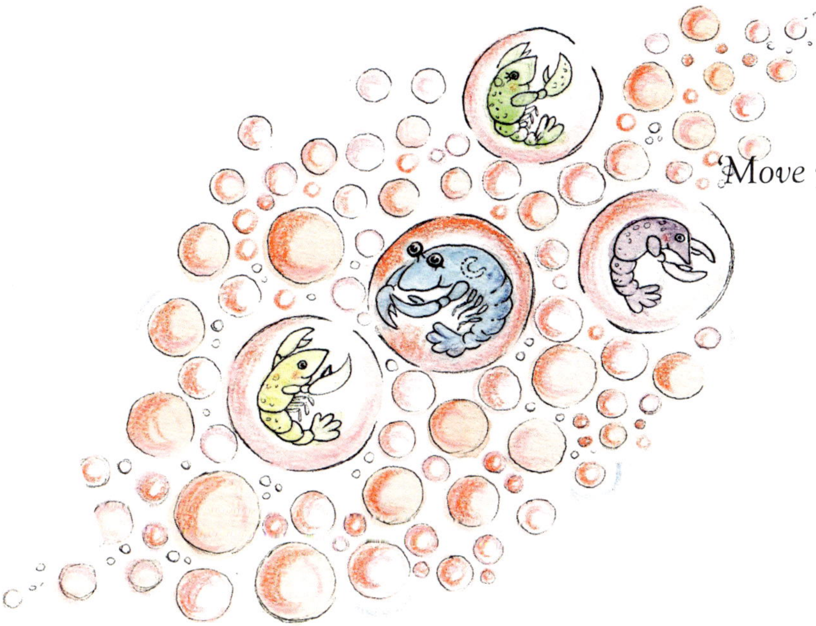

'My mum' said Claude, *'the Duchess; don't ask, everybody calls her the Duchess round this neck of the rocks, it's a long story but it's something to do with her royal wiggle and bossy nature. Anyway, she tells me I've got 4,000 brothers and sisters – that would probably explain the noise then!'*

'Oh, mum's on the move again – she can smell with her feet you know, so no doubt we're on the trail of a smelly breakfast.'

'Mum's getting frustrated, she can see the food but can't get to it, oh wait, she's found a way in.'

'Breathe in kids, we're going in' said the Duchess.

'Just one more pot Max' said Pops *'and we can head back to Padstow in time for lunch'*. The last pot was particularly heavy, it took both Pops and Max to pull it aboard and there before them was the Duchess in all her glory. The biggest and most spectacular lobster Max had ever seen.

'She's a beauty', said Pops, *'she must be 50 or 60 years old and she's laden with eggs. I bet she's got some stories to tell'*. She had beautiful blue, green and white markings, bright blue claws and she was covered in tiny barnacles.

ENTRANCE
PADSTOW
PADSTOW
PADSTOW
PADSTO

'I know exactly what we'll do with this beauty. We can take her to the Lobster Hatchery; Tinker will be really pleased to take care of her and her babies and then you'll be able to see them all whenever you like.'

This sounds exciting, thought Max.

'Let's put her in the tank and take her back to Padstow' said Pops.

It wasn't long before Max and Pops arrived at the hatchery. Tinker was sat on the harbour wall, just about to take a bite out of his pasty when he saw them approaching with a big box of water and giant claws sticking out of the top.

When Tinker saw the Duchess, he jumped with joy and did a little jig;

'What has the sea brought in today,
a berried hen lobster about to lay,
the patter of tiny lobster feet,
what a delight and fisherman's treat'.

'*Fantastic!*' said Tinker, '*our first lobster to start off the season and she's got a good brood of healthy eggs. The Duchess and her young will be safe here in the hatchery and because they're away from all the predators in the sea, more of her babies will survive. Once they hatch you can come and help feed them if you like Max, and watch them grow*'.

This all sounded very good news for Duchess. She was relieved to think that her young had the best chance in life and she became quite fond of Tinker and Max, peering over the tank during the next few months.

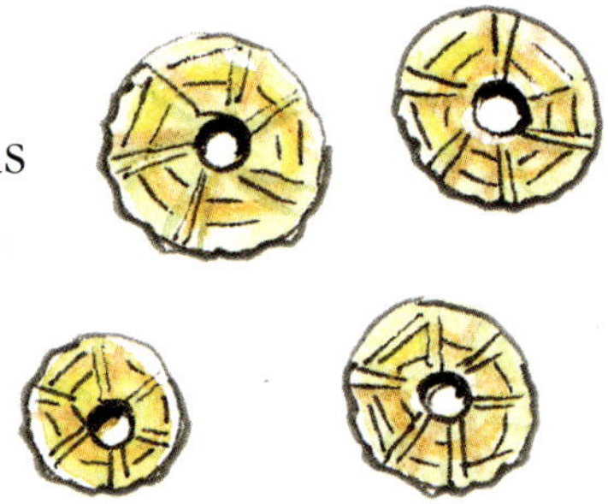

Claude, Squat, Wriggle and Titch were getting very fidgety and raucous while the Duchess dreamt of a minute's peace and quiet. Tonight is the night she thought, a new moon and excitable babies ready to start their own journey.

She waited until it was quiet and dark. Tinker had locked up and gone home. The Duchess crawled out of her shelter, stretched out her eight legs, lifted her tail up and started to shake, wriggle and splash. As she did, the baby lobsters launched from their eggs and took their first float up to the surface.

'Look at me' said Claude, *'I can flip and flap without Squat's head sticking in my side, or Wriggle's smelly feet in my face'*. *'Whoopeee!'* cried Claude as he did a somersault.

Some of the other mother lobsters in the tank were grumbling about the noise, but couldn't be heard over the thousands of happy baby lobsters. It was going to be a long night. It took five nights for all 4,001 babies to hatch.

'Quick, hide!' shouted Wriggle, as Tinker peered over the tank but it was too late, they were caught in a net and the next thing they knew, they were swirling around with the bubbles.

'This is cool!' shouted Squat as he whooshed past Claude at high speed.

Each day the baby lobsters got bigger and bigger, and occasionally they would get so fat they would break out of their hard outer shell, just to grow a bigger and better one; until one day their new shell came with **proper claws**! It was like graduating from school, all set up and ready for the big wide world and food that you could really dig your claws into!

Only, now that Claude had claws, he kept hurting his brothers and sisters by being too rough and on the quiet, occasionally even thought about eating them. This was not something Claude was comfortable with, not after all they had been through together.

Tinker knew that this was actually quite normal for a lobster, so as soon as the little lobsters grew claws they were netted out again and separated into little tanks of their own. It was a good chance for Claude to build some independence ready for the off.

Three months went past, Claude, Squat, Wriggle and Titch grew stronger and stronger. They were ready to find their feet on the ocean floor, excited about finding their own burrow and sampling the delights of all the different foods that happened to walk past their territory.

Tinker had arranged for Pops and Max to release the Duchess and her young lobsters back into the wild.

Max and Pops said goodbye to Claude, Squat, Wriggle, Titch and all the other baby lobsters before they lowered the old lobster pot back to the ocean floor.

When the coast was clear, one by one, they crawled out of the pot, set all eight feet onto the seabed and looked around in awe of all the activity going on around them.

Claude looked up at the waves above and said excitedly,

'we're home again'.

Titch piped up, *'smells good Squat, I can smell molluscs in that direction with my left, second foot and fish in that direction with my right, third foot. Let's go!'.* They all headed off in different directions, perhaps they will meet again one day.

Before letting Duchess go, Pops marked her with a 'V notch' on her tail. This is a mark that is used by fishermen to indicate that she is a breeding female and so she can continue to add to the lobster population. Fishermen are not allowed to keep a V-notched lobster so the Duchess was safe.

The Duchess found a lovely snug cave where she settled down for a quiet nap. '*Peace at last*' she thought. She didn't have a care in the world, well except for wondering what Claude, Squat, Wriggle and Titch were up to, not to mention her other hundreds of baby lobsters.

And I can tell you,

they did get up to lots of

mischief,

but that's

another story ....

LOBSTER FACTS did you know ....

The biggest lobster ever recorded weighed 20kg and stretched to 106cm, caught off eastern Canada in 1977.

Lobsters are highly cannibalistic, they will eat each other given the chance.

Lobsters have one crushing claw and one slicing claw and can be left or right handed.

Lobsters take 5 to 7 years to reach market size,

A female will carry between 5,000 and 40,000 eggs on the underside of her tail for up to 12 months before they hatch.

There are 138 species of lobster with some really curious names; Musical Furry Lobster, Shield Fan Lobster, Scorpion Mud Lobster, African Spear Lobster, Buffalo Blunt-horn Lobster just to name a few.

Lobsters can live to 100 years old.

Lobsters have 3 stomachs.

Lobsters often lose limbs during moulting or battles but they are able to regenerate most appendages, except for the eye. However, appendages may appear in the eyes place, an unwanted foot perhaps!

A lobster's hard outer shell is called an exoskeleton, which means they have an external skeleton.

Lobsters date back to the Devonian period, an incredible 400 million years ago!

There's nothing better than watching my two boys' eyes light up when I pull up our lobster pot onto the fishing boat and see what the ocean has brought us today. It's never the same twice. They are both fanatical about rock pooling and anything that lives and breathes.

In our lifetime, those that have been intimate with the ocean have seen a huge change in flora and fauna. Wouldn't it be nice if there was a healthy and diverse fishery for our children when they grow up? It's a world worth looking after and exploring.

Sarah Boothroyd, Author

Painting drawing and illustration is such an important part of my life and my ideas are constantly stimulated and fed by the beautiful environment I live in. The North coast of Cornwall is exceptional with it's dramatic coastline which is a perfect home for lobsters. I love the way these incredible crustaceans reflect this in their colouring and patterning. Each one is so different and seem to have a character of their own, which is what I try to capture.

Caroline Cleave, Illustrator

The National Lobster Hatchery

Fishing is a traditional way of life in Cornwall and many coastal communities still rely on shellfish; not just the fishermen and their families but the seafood restaurants, cafes, fishmongers, related retail and tourism that attracts visitors to our quaint little Cornish harbours.

The Norwegian lobster fishery collapsed between 1960 and 1980 and has never recovered. In the late 1980's, early 1990's the fishery around Cornwall and the Isles of Scilly saw a decline in catch. Cornwall Sea Fisheries Committee, (responsible for fisheries management out to six miles), decided to take a multi-dimensional and proactive approach to safeguard the future of the fishery. They closed the fishery for egg bearing female lobsters and increased the minimum landing size. As an additional safeguard The National Lobster Hatchery was also set up in 2000. We became a charity in 2004, to feed juvenile lobsters back into the fishery at the other end.

Comparatively very little is known about the European lobster. Research is constantly underway at the hatchery, to understand more about these amazing creatures, their nutritional requirements, their lifecycle and behaviour and the environmental issues that threaten their future.